Royal Fireworks Language Arts

Building POEMS

Second Edition

Michael Clay Thompson

Royal Fireworks Press
UNIONVILLE, NEW YORK

October 2022

Royal Fireworks Press
41 First Avenue, P.O. Box 399
Unionville, NY 10988-0399
(845) 726-4444
fax: (845) 726-3824
email: mail@rfwp.com
website: rfwp.com

ISBN: 978-0-89824-708-4

Design and graphics: Michael Clay Thompson
Publisher: Dr. T.M. Kemnitz
Editor: Jennifer Ault
Cover design: Kerri Ann Ruhl

Printed and bound in Unionville, New York,
at the Royal Fireworks facility. 13o22

About the cover: The front cover is Bodiam Castle in East Sussex, England. It was built during a short period from 1385 to the early 1390s. The site was selected for the castle, and it was planned with the moat, which is artificial and entirely surrounds the building. It is one the best-preserved fourteenth-century castles in the United Kingdom. Situated in the Sussex countryside, it is now a lovely, peaceful site.

The back cover is the Santa Maria del Fiore cathedral in Florence. It was designed in the fourteenth century, and building began without anyone having a clear idea how the proposed dome would be built. In 1418 a competition was held to solve the problem of building the dome. Filippo Brunelleschi (1377-1446) won, and he spent most of the rest of his life in the construction of the dome, which is the largest brick dome in the world. His design was an octagonal one that required more than four million bricks to complete. He had to invent a new hoist to get the bricks and mortar to where they were needed.

Photographs by Dr. Thomas Milton Kemnitz.

Table of Contents

We make buildings strong to resist
the wind, but why do we make
them beautiful?

Building Poems

We are the builders.
We are the makers.
Human beings make things.

Beautiful things.

We build with wood, glass, concrete, steel—
and we build with words.

The things we make—whether they are buildings or poems—have parts, and the parts fit, and they are arranged in a pattern for a purpose.

Like a glass tower that reflects the sky—that almost becomes part of the sky—a poem is built—with poem pieces.
A poem is a kind of building.

Brunelleschi's Dome

In 1418 Filippo Brunelleschi,
a grumpy architect from Florence, Italy,
was challenged to build
an enormous dome above the cathedral
of Santa Maria del Fiore in Florence.

No one knew how to do it.

Even Lorenzo Ghiberti,
who had cast the great bronze doors
of Florence's Baptistery of San Giovanni,
could not do it.

The opening that the dome would
have to cover was huge—impossible—
138 feet across, and the walls
that would support the base of the dome
were 180 feet high—a long fall.

But Brunelleschi designed a hollow dome,
two dome-shells with space in between,
made of bricks in a strong herringbone pattern.

After six centuries
his dome still stands.

Like Brunelleschi,
poets solve problems,
but poets do not make
domes of brick. They build
domes of words,
arranging sounds
to confirm the meanings of ideas.

Poets use the sounds of words
as building materials.

When Thomas Hardy wanted
to describe thorny vines on a freezing day,
he used scratchy sounds—
k, *sk*, *st*, *t*, and *g*!

The tangled bine-stems
scored the sky
Like strings of broken lyres...

The *k*'s and *g*'s in English words can sound scratchy and rough, but if they are present in a line full of soft sounds, such as *l*'s, *m*'s, *n*'s, *f*'s, and *v*'s, they can lose their sting. Here is a line of poetry from William Shakespeare's play *Romeo and Juliet*. When Juliet's mother asks her if she can like Count Paris, Juliet, who really does not like Count Paris, answers her mother:

I'll look to like,
if looking liking move.

In other words, "I'll try to like him, if trying can move me to like him"! Even though there are some *k*'s in Juliet's words, the line is soft; the *k*'s absorb the softness of the rest of the sentence. Why do *f*'s and *v*'s sound soft? How are those two sounds different from one another?

like

if move

ook

liking

oking

When we think
about the sounds in our words,
we realize that each sound
has its own spirit.
Sounds are like little creatures.
Some sounds stop,
like *t* or *d*.
Some sounds continue,
like *v* or *f*.
Some sounds pound,
like *b* and *d*,
and some sounds murmur,
like *m* and *n*.
Some sounds, like *g* and *k*, are hard
and rough, and some sounds
are soft, like *l* and *r*.
There are sounds full of air,
like *f* and *s*, and sounds
that have air and voice,
like *v*. An *f* is like a *v*
without a voice. Notice
that you can shift from *f*
to *v* just by adding your voice!

(Some words, like
buzz and *crash*, sound
like the noises they
stand for. This is called
onomatopoeia.)

dbdbdbdb

mmmmmmmmmmmmmmmmmmmmmm

We use letters
to put word sounds on paper.
There are twenty-six letters,
but there are more
sounds than that because some
letters make more than one
sound and because letters
combine. The sound *th*
is different from either
t or *h*, and the *th* in *think*
is different from the *th* in *those*.

There are two kinds of letters:
vowels and consonants.

The **vowels** are the open
voice sounds a e i o u and
sometimes y.

The **consonants** are the
clicks and buzzes and
percussion sounds
b c d f g h j k l m n p q r s t
v w x z.

a e i o u a e i o u a e i o u a e i o u a e i o u a e i o u a ether

ther

ghklmnpqrstvwxzlmnpqrstvwxzbdcfghklmnpqrstvwxzbdcf

ouaeiouaeiouaeiouaeiaeiouaeiouae

We use the letter *a*
to represent several sounds
in English.

There is the ah *a* of *father*,
the ay *a* of *snake*,
the aah *a* of *smash*,
and the uh *a*
of *maternal*.

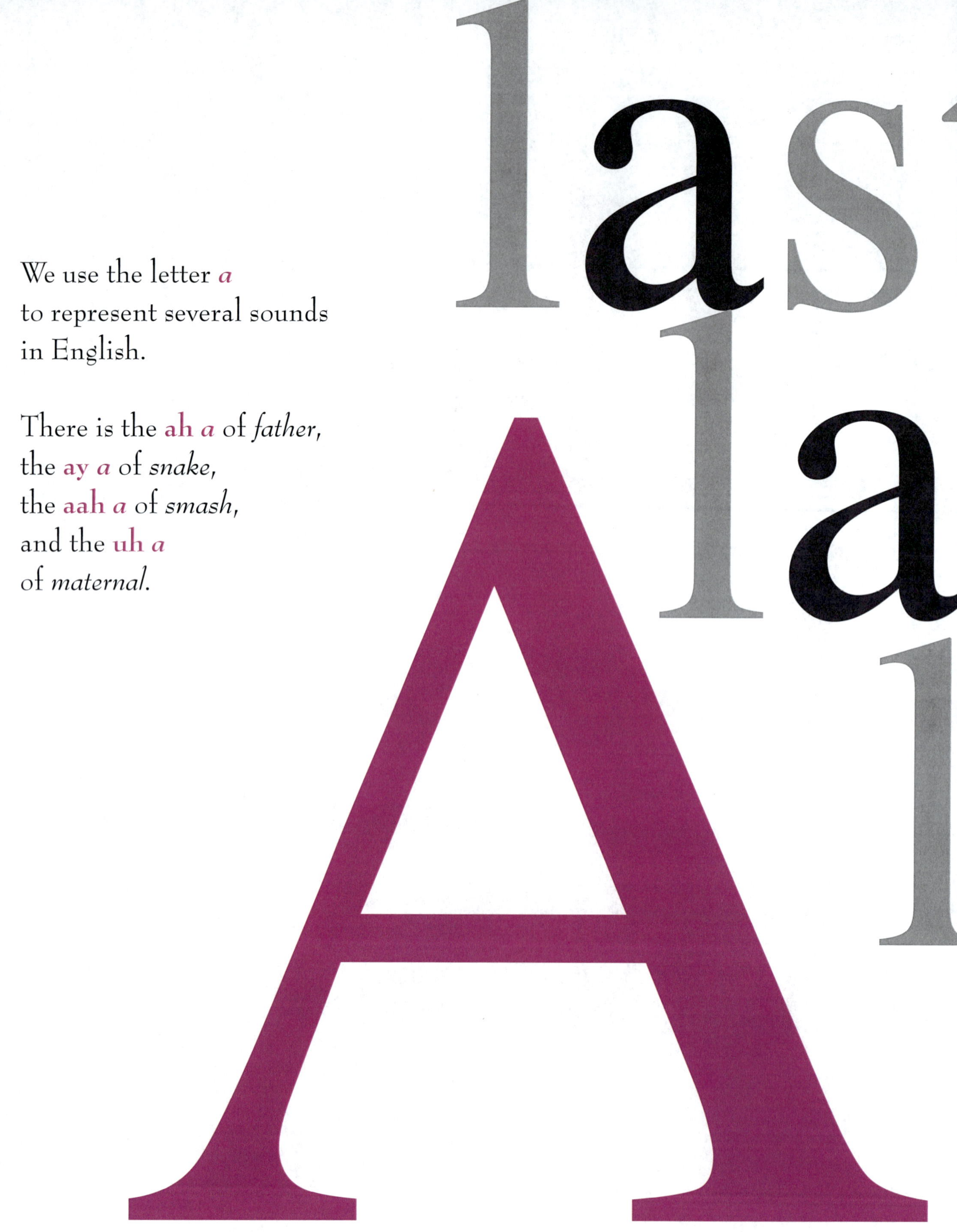

sagna
ate
lanky

PATTERNS
alliteration
assonance
rhyme
consonanc

1
OF SOUND

PATTERNS

One thing to do with sounds
is to repeat them in patterns.
There are different ways to
repeat sounds.

When words end
in the same sound, like
flake and *ache*, that is **rhyme**.

When words begin with
the same sound, like
moon, *milk*, and *meanie*,
that is called **alliteration**.

When words share the
same vowel sound, like
croon, *dupe*, and *newt*,
that is **assonance**.

And when words share
the same consonant sound, like
begin, *aghast*, *snuggle*, and *rigging*,
that is called **consonance**.

d c d e f e f
syrup
laugh
stirrup
half
foot lost loop
sunny
season
sassy
sunken
cereal
serious
silly
soupy
soul

Rhyme, words that end alike,
is one of the most important
techniques in poetry.

When poets put the rhymes
at the ends of the lines,
that is called end rhyme.
There are wonderful end rhymes
in Lewis Carroll's *Alice in Wonderland*:

"You are old, Father William," the young man said,
"And your hair has become very white,
And yet you incessantly stand on your head—
Do you think, at your age, it is right?"

"In my youth," Father William replied to his son,
"I feared it might injure the brain;
But, now that I'm perfectly sure I have none,
Why, I do it again and again."

end

s lakes said white head right son brain none again falls walls shal

When the rhymes are inside the lines,
that is called internal rhyme.
Alfred, Lord Tennyson, used
internal rhyme in his poem "The Splendor Falls":

The splendor **falls** on castle **walls**
And snowy summits old in story;
The long light **shakes** across the **lakes**,
And the wild cataract leaps in glory.

internal rhyme

Simple Simon met a pieman...

lakes said white head right son brain none again falls walls shake

When the rhyme looks the same
but does not sound the same,
that is called **eye rhyme**.
The British poet Thomas Hardy
used this eye rhyme in his poem
"The Darkling Thrush":

At once a voice arose am**ong**
The bleak twigs overhead
In a fullhearted evens**ong**
Of joy illimited.

Among and *evensong* are eye rhyme because
they rhyme only to the eye!
They look like rhymes, but they do not
end with the same sounds.

een tough though rain again sand thousand how below not depot worry s

rhyme

beak steak moss gross flower grower hour pour edge knowledge frown gr

ALLITERATI

Six Caryatids
of the Erechtheion

Michael Clay Thompson

Parthenon dawn drops.
Stormlight shocks the rock acropolis,
rubble fallen, all in gray,
waking woman-columns—
stone stares open, solemn,
guarding the child-grief
of Artemis, artless goddess
of the wild.

Let's think about rhymes....
Where are rhymes?
They are at the ends of words.

But poets do not have to work
at the ends of words.
They can also work at
the beginnings.

Repeating a sound at the
beginnings of words, as in
"Fe, fi, fo, fum" or
"Peter Piper picked a peck of pickled peppers"
is **alliteration**.

In *Alice in Wonderland*,
Lewis Carroll used alliteration
on the *j* consonant sound
so subtly that it is difficult to spot:

> How doth the little crocodile
> Improve his shining tail,
> And pour the waters of the Nile
> On every golden scale!
>
> How cheerfully he seems to grin,
> How neatly spreads his claws,
> And welcomes little fishes in
> With gently smiling jaws!

If **rhymes** are at the ends of words,
such as *flute*, *root*, and *suit*,
and **alliteration** is at the beginnings of words,
such as *Simple Simon*,
then what else can we do with sound?

We can repeat vowel and consonant sounds in the middles of words. When we repeat a vowel sound, that is called **assonance**, and when we repeat a consonant sound, that is called **consonance**.

For example, *fish*, *dish*, and *wish* are rhymes,
but *fish*, *lift*, *miss*, and *blip* are assonance.
Carl Sandburg used assonance in his poem "Splinter"
to describe the pretty song of the cricket:

It is so thin a splinter of singing.

The words *it*, *is*, *thin*, *splinter*, and *singing* are not rhymes because they do not end the same way. All they do is repeat the *i* sound, and that is assonance.

ASSON

Assonance can be hard to spot
if the vowel sound is spelled in different ways.
Poet X.J. Kennedy, in his "Little Elegy,"
used assonance in

Earth whose *circles* round us skim....

In her poem "The Moon and the Yew Tree,"
Sylvia Plath used ghostly assonance to enhance the *ooo*
sound of *moon* and *yew*:

The moon is my mother...
Her blue garments unloose small
bats and owls.

ance

The repetition of consonant sounds is called **consonance**.

T.S. Eliot used consonance to repeat the *sh* sound in his poem "Preludes":

> ...and eyes
> Assured of certain certainties,
> The conscience of a blackened street
> Impatient to assume the world.

Notice that the *sh* sound is spelled three different ways in the three words *assured, conscience,* and *impatient*. This makes it hard to catch Eliot using his poetic technique. Modern poets often hide their methods and try to make their poems sound natural and spontaneous, when the poems are actually careful works of art.

sh

nance

The British poet Percy Bysshe Shelley, the husband of Mary Shelley (the author of *Frankenstein*), wrote these lines in his poem "England in 1819." Look for the alliteration, end rhyme, and assonance.

An old, mad, blind, despised, and dying king,
Princes, the dregs of their dull race, who flow
Through public scorn,—mud from a muddy spring,—
Rulers who neither see, nor feel, nor know

A nice alliteration in "nor know," don't you think? Shelley combined alliteration and consonance to stress the pounding *d* sound:

old mad blind despised and dying
dregs dull mud muddy

And he used subtle assonance that almost goes unnoticed:

spring neither see feel

Sh

old mad blind despised and dying dregs dull mud muddy old mad blind despised and dying dregs dull mud muddy old mad blind despised and dying dregs dull mud muddy old mad blind despised and dying dregs dull mud muddy old mad blind despised and dying dregs dull mud muddy old mad blind despised and dying dregs dull mud muddy old mad blind despised mud

elley

John Augustus Roebling's Brooklyn Bridge

Michael Clay Thompson

He built the Brooklyn Bridge,
complete, in eighteen eighty-three—a neat
three thousand four hundred sixty feet—
spanning old East River's flow,
soaring over boats and barges,
in suspense, stone Gothic arches,
towers, cables, wire wings,
power-strung instrument strings,
moaning low in winter wind,
crowds of people walking in,
City looming just ahead; when
walking, driving, crossing now,
it's all connected—bridged somehow.
If the bridge does not start wobbling,
thanks be to Augustus Roebling.

I
ne
ver
saw
a
pur

le
cow
2
meter

Words have rhythm.

When we speak, we give more emphasis
to some words or parts of words than to others.
We stress sounds by pronouncing them with
a higher volume and with more firmness.

We say CHICKen, not chickEN.

We say baNAna, not banaNA.

By controlling the pattern of stressed and unstressed
syllables in poems, poets can create regular
rhythm, called meter. They do this by
using small units of meter;
each unit is called a foot.

foot

The American poet Gelett Burgess,
who was born in 1863,
is remembered for one poem.
Look at the stressed syllables, in
purple, and notice how he arranged
the patterns of stress into a regular meter:

I never saw a purple cow,
I never hope to see one;
But I can tell you, anyhow,
I'd rather see than be one.

Did you notice the way Burgess alternated between unstressed and stressed syllables? Every other syllable is stressed. We could say that the pattern in this poem is a two-syllable pattern, with an unstressed syllable followed by a stressed syllable.

A two-syllable foot with the stress on the second syllable is called an iamb.

If we broke Burgess's poem into its iambs
and put slashes between the feet,
it would look like this:

I ne / ver saw / a pur / ple cow,
I ne / ver hope / to see / one;
But I / can tell / you, an / y how,
I'd ra / ther see / than be / one.

Notice that the foot is made up of syllables; "ver saw" is an iambic foot, and "a pur" is an iambic foot. When we talk about the poetic foot, we are only thinking about the pattern of stresses, not about the words. A foot can be part of a long word, or the end of one word with the beginning of the next.

Notice that Burgess's poem has four iambs in the first and third lines. Four iambs per line are called

iambic tetrameter.

Notice, too, that lines two and four have three iambs followed by a single unstressed syllable. When we add a final unstressed syllable this way, it is called a **feminine ending**.

There are four main kinds of foot in English poetry. They are called the iamb, the trochee (pronounced TROkee), the dactyl, and the anapest.

The iamb and trochee have two syllables. In an iamb the stress is on the second syllable, and in a trochee the stress is on the first.

The dactyl and the anapest each have three syllables. In a dactyl the stress is on the first syllable, and in an anapest the stress is on the third.

iamb

There was a crooked man...he went a crooked mile.
The Queen of Hearts, she made some tarts...
I do not like thee, Doctor Fell; the reason why I cannot tell.

trochee

Barber, barber, shave a pig...
Mary, Mary, quite contrary...
Peter Piper picked a peck of pickled peppers.

dactyl

Hickory, dickory...
Home again, home again, jiggety...
Ladybird, ladybird, fly away...

anapest

an old woman who lived in a shoe
an old lady upon a white horse
there I met an old man

There are many who say
that a dog has his day.
(Dylan Thomas)

Notice that each of the traditional kinds of poetic foot has only one stressed syllable:

sp

Sometimes, poets stress two syllables (or maybe more) in a row in order to make something stand out. A poetic foot with two stressed syllables is called a spondee.

And a merry old soul was he.

This is the house that Jack built.

ondee

Emily Dickinson used a spondee in her poem "XCVII," which is mostly iambic:

To make a prairie it takes a clover
and one bee,—
One clover, and a bee,
and revery.
The revery alone will do
If bees are few.

alo

Do you see how Dickinson's spondee emphasizes the thought that a single bee can start a great natural process?

If bee

The re /

very /

ne / will do

s / are few.

William Blake alternated iambic lines and trochaic lines in his poem "A Poison Tree." If we put the stressed syllables in purple, we see that lines one and three are trochaic, and lines two and four are iambic:

I was angry with my friend:
I told my wrath, my wrath did end.
I was angry with my foe:
I told it not; my wrath did grow.

Notice that Blake dropped the final unstressed syllable of the fourth trochee in lines one and three. By doing this, he could end the line on a stress, creating a rhythm that sounds like

BA da BA da BA da BOOM.

We can see from this that a poem does not have to use the same meter in every line, even though most poems do.

Most poems have from one to eight feet per line.
For example, many poems are written with five iambs per line.
In William Shakespeare's play *Romeo and Juliet*, when Romeo first sees Juliet, he exclaims to himself,

O, she doth teach the torches to burn bright!

It is five perfect iambs:

O, she / doth teach / the tor / ches to / burn bright!

The English language is naturally iambic. We tend to speak in iambs naturally. For this reason, poets use iambs for noble characters and good news, and they often use trochees—anti-iambs—for evil and for villains. Shakespeare used trochees for the witches' chant in *Macbeth* as they danced around the poisoned cauldron (he dropped the final unstressed syllable in the fourth trochee of these lines):

Adder's / fork, and / blind-worm's / sting
Lizard's / leg, and / owlet's / wing...

On October 25, 1854, 673 British cavalry soldiers charged entrenched Russian cannons at Balaclava, in the Crimea. Few soldiers survived. It was one of the most heroic charges in history. In "The Charge of the Light Brigade" the British poet Alfred, Lord Tennyson, used dactyls to express the sound of hoofbeats. BAdada BAdada... Notice that Tennyson dropped an unstressed syllable from lines two, four, and six, and he ended lines three and seven with a single stressed syllable. By varying from strict dactylic meter, he increased the drama.

Half a league, half a league
Half a league onward,
All in the valley of Death
Rode the six hundred.
"Forward the Light Brigade!
Charge for the guns!" he said.
Into the valley of Death
Rode the six hundred.

Tennyson used two dactyls per line
as the basic form of his poem.
Two dactyls per line is called dactylic dimeter.
The names of the meters, based on
how many poetic feet there are in each line, are:

one - **monometer**
two - **dimeter**
three - **trimeter**
four - **tetrameter**
five - **pentameter**
six - **hexameter**
seven - **heptameter**
eight - **octameter**

For example, a line of trochaic tetrameter has four trochees:

1 2 3 4
Double, / double, / toil and / trouble...

A line of iambic pentameter has five iambs.
Shakespeare used iambic pentameter
for King Henry's inspiring speech in *Henry V*:

For he to-day that sheds his blood with me
Shall be my brother; be he ne'er so vile,
This day shall gentle his condition:
And gentlemen in England now a-bed
Shall think themselves accursed they were not here...

Robert Louis Stevenson, who wrote the novel *Treasure Island,* also wrote poems for children. He used iambic tetrameter for his poem "The Sun's Travels":

The sun is not a-bed, when I
At night upon my pillow lie;
Still round the earth his way he takes,
And morning after morning makes.

While here at home, in shining day,
We round the sunny garden play,
Each little Indian sleepy-head
Is being kissed and put to bed.

And when at eve I rise from tea,
Day dawns beyond the Atlantic Sea;
And all the children in the west
Are getting up and being dressed.

Stevenson's poem is a good display of meter. We see clearly that the poetic feet are not the same as the words. An iamb might be made of the end of one word and the beginning of the next!

And morn / ing af / ter morn / ing makes.

af

flocks
locked
talks
top
dropped
block
box
locked
rocks
stalklike

Giuseppi, Verde

Michael Clay Thompson

Giuseppi built the wall with rocks,
and knocked them into spaces.
He worked all morning; flocks
of geese passed over, shadows tracing
mocking goose grays on the ground. His green
box—crammed with hammers, maces—
green box, *verde*, full of tools, their handles
stalklike, smooth.... He worked, no talks, just traced
the wall out in his brain, and dropped the stones
on top, and finally up the wall rose, up
to window height. The window stood upright
against the tree, an old window from grandpa's
house—torn down, a ruin, the beams
like bones admitting light, amazing.
Giuseppi braced the window on the wall, and locked
it into place with bricks, old bricks
from his grandfather's basement, strong cement
to block the window in.
Lunch time. Giuseppi walked, a shady place,
he ate his sandwich carefully, small bites,
and looking, liked the brick-locked window,
with—now—its old life new...
and he would paint it green, *verde*, not blue.

Let's have some fun with meter!

We have learned that there are four traditional kinds of meter: iambs, trochees, dactyls, and anapests. We also learned that a spondee is two stressed syllables in a row.

We learned about end rhyme, internal rhyme, and eye rhyme, as well as assonance, consonance, and alliteration.

See if you can write four four-line poems, one in each meter, using some of the sound controls in each poem. The lines should be either tetrameter or pentameter.

Pick a topic and four words that will appear in each of the four poems.

It is okay to be humorous or playful.

For example, if we were to have a topic of curiosity and the four words *chicken*, *blues*, *flip*, and *mouse*....

The Chicken Blues, in Four Parts

Michael Clay Thompson

iambic pentameter

She flipped the chicken over seekin' for
the measly mouse, but no—where could it be?
The news gave hews of blues to Elinor,
and chickens are no help; they squawk, you see.

trochaic tetrameter

Fiendish chickens charged the pantry,
Crashing 'gainst the doors—no entry;
Chanting war cries, Sousa's blues, and
Even Bob the Mouse flipped out, man.

dactylic tetrameter

What could the chickens be thinking, he wondered as
Hundreds of cluckings arose in the kitchen, but
Suddenly Muncey the mouse got the blues—it was
Evident someone was flipping the halibut.

anapestic pentameter

At the rear of the chicken, white feathers stuck out like a fan.
At the front of the chicken, a tune like a croon...like the blues.
To the left of the chicken, the mouse did a rough flip on sand.
To the right of the chicken, a hiccough sat up from a snooze.

Knowing what we know now, if we were to examine a well-known poem, what might we see?

The Eagle

Alfred, Lord Tennyson

He clasps the crag with crooked hands; a
Close to the sun in lonely lands, a
Ringed with the azure world, he stands. a

The wrinkled sea beneath him crawls; b
He watches from his mountain walls, b
And like a thunderbolt he falls. b

We would see assonance:

clasp, crag, hands, azure, lands
ringed, wrinkled; sea, beneath; azure world

We would see consonance:

crooked, wrinkled, like (these support the alliterated *k* sound)

We would see alliteration:

clasps, crag, crooked, close, crawls; ringed, wrinkled
watches, walls; lonely lands

We would notice that the power and claws of the eagle are described with sharp *k* and *g* sounds:

clasp, crag, crooked

We would see a spondee:

he falls

We would see that the poem has end rhyme:

hands, lands, stands
crawls, walls, falls

When we study the rhymes of a poem, we usually show how the rhyme scheme works by assigning the letter *a* to the first rhyme, and the letter *b* to the second rhyme, and so forth. The rhyme scheme of Tennyson's poem is *aaa bbb*. A ballad has a rhyme scheme of *abcb*.

We would see that the meter of the poem is iambic tetrameter:

He clasps / the crag / with crook / ed hands

Finally, we would notice that the poem is in two parts—two three-line sections. Lots of poems have these sections. A section might be three lines, as we see here, or it might be four lines, with rhyme scheme *aabb* or even *abab*. These sections of poems are called stanzas.

Tennyson's poem has two three-line stanzas.

wls, crag, crooked, close, crawls, l

LXXX

Emily Dickinson

The sky is low, the clouds are mean, a
A traveling flake of snow b
Across a barn or through a rut c
Debates if it will go. b

A narrow wind complains all day d
How some one treated him; e
Nature, like us, is sometimes caught f
Without her diadem. e

stanza 3

STANZA

The English word *stanza* comes
from the Italian *stanza*, a room.
The Italians got *stanza* from the Latin verb
stare, to stand. The idea is that a stanza
is like a room, a part of a larger building,
a place where we can stand, stop, stay.

A stanza is a section of a poem.
Poets build poems out of stanzas,
as architects build buildings out of floors.

Stanzas are sometimes named for the number of lines they contain:

couplet: a two-line stanza
triplet: a three-line stanza
quatrain: a four-line stanza
quintet: a five-line stanza
sestet: a six-line stanza

There is also a ballad stanza, which is a quatrain,
four lines, *abcb*, in which lines one and three are
iambic tetrameter, and lines two and four
are iambic trimeter. Emily Dickinson used
the ballad stanza for her poem "LII"
(we number Dickinson's poems with Roman
numerals):

LII
Emily Dickinson

New feet within my garden go,
New fingers stir the sod;
A troubador upon the elm
Betrays the solitude.

New children play upon the green,
New weary sleep below;
And still the pensive spring returns,
And still the punctual snow!

New feet / within / my gar / den go,
New fin / gers stir / the sod;
A trou / bador / upon / the elm
Betrays / the sol / itude.

SONNET

An Italian sonnet is an octave and a sestet, *abbaabba cdecde*. It was Thomas Wyatt the Elder who introduced the Italian sonnet into English poetry. William Shakespeare developed the sonnet so much that it acquired its own name: an English sonnet is three quatrains and a couplet, *abab cdcd efef gg*.

In 1816 the English poet John Keats wrote this variation of an Italian sonnet after staying up all night reading George Chapman's new translation of Homer's *The Iliad*. The poem says, essentially, I have read much, but I have never understood Homer until I read Chapman; then, I felt like an astronomer discovering a new planet, or like Cortez (it was actually Balboa) and his men discovering the Pacific Ocean and realizing that they had just discovered the back side of the world!

Much have I travell'd in the realms of gold,	a
And many goodly states and kingdoms seen;	b
Round many western islands have I been	b
Which bards in fealty to Apollo hold.	a
Oft of one wide expanse had I been told	a
That deep-brow'd Homer ruled as his demesne;	c
Yet did I never breathe its pure serene	c
Till I heard Chapman speak out loud and bold:	a
Then felt I like some watcher of the skies	d
When a new planet swims into his ken;	e
Or like stout Cortez when with eagle eyes	d
He star'd at the Pacific—and all his men	e
Look'd at each other with a wild surmise—	d
Silent, upon a peak in Darien.	e

RIME ROYAL

The rime royal stanza is seven lines of iambic pentameter, *ababbcc*. It was first developed in English poetry by Geoffrey Chaucer but became known as royal when King James I of Scotland used it. William Wordsworth wrote this stanza of rime royal (the full poem has 20 rime royal stanzas, 140 lines):

There was roaring in the wind all night; a
The rain came heavily and down in floods; b
But now the sun is rising calm and bright. a
The birds are singing in the distant woods; b
Over his own sweet voice the stockdove broods; b
The jay makes answer as the magpie chatters; c
And the air is filled with pleasant noise of waters. c

night
floods
bright
woods
broods
chatters
waters

Domicile, in Rime Royal
Michael Clay Thompson

The house was made to overlook the sea,
with plaster walls, built tight against the wind.
The winter storm would howl and roar, but she
was warm inside, and then she would pretend
that he was home—not out there—once again.
For months his fishing fleet would be from home,
and she would wait—a sea-fate still unknown.

7

LIMERICK

A limerick is a five-line nonsense poem that is mostly anapest, with a rhyme scheme *aabba*. Lines one, two, and five have three feet, but lines three and four have only two feet. The most famous limerick poet is undoubtedly Edward Lear (1812-1888), who wrote this limerick (The town of Nice is pronounced *niece*):

There was an old person of Nice,	a
Whose associates were usually Geese.	a
They walked out together,	b
In all sorts of weather.	b
That affable person of Nice!	a

Here is another of Lear's limericks:

There was an old man on the Border,	a
Who lived in the utmost disorder;	a
He danced with the cat,	b
And made tea in his hat,	b
Which vexed all the folks on the Border.	a

If we were to write a limerick about a barnyard animal and use an eye rhyme in it, it might come out like this (sorry to keep harping on chickens):

A sickening chicken named Hannah,
She slipped all the time on banana.
When she bought surer shoes,
She developed bad toes—
This story's pure Americana.

Notice that the first foot of the first line is usually an iamb, not an anapest, and that there is an extra unstressed syllable at the end of the line. The two middle feet are correct anapests:

A sick / ening chick / en named Han / nah

anapest

Here is a poem by Emily Dickinson.

Let's see how many things we can notice about it.
First, look closely at the poem on this page,
and then look at details on the next page.

CXI
Emily Dickinson

A door just opened on a street—
I, lost, was passing by—
An instant's width of warmth disclosed,
And wealth, and company.

The door as sudden shut, and I,
I, lost, was passing by,—
Lost doubly, but by contrast most,
Enlightening misery.

If Dickinson is not talking
about a real door, but about
something else, then
what is she talking about?

subtle sounds
sudden shut and
contrast most
instant width disclosed

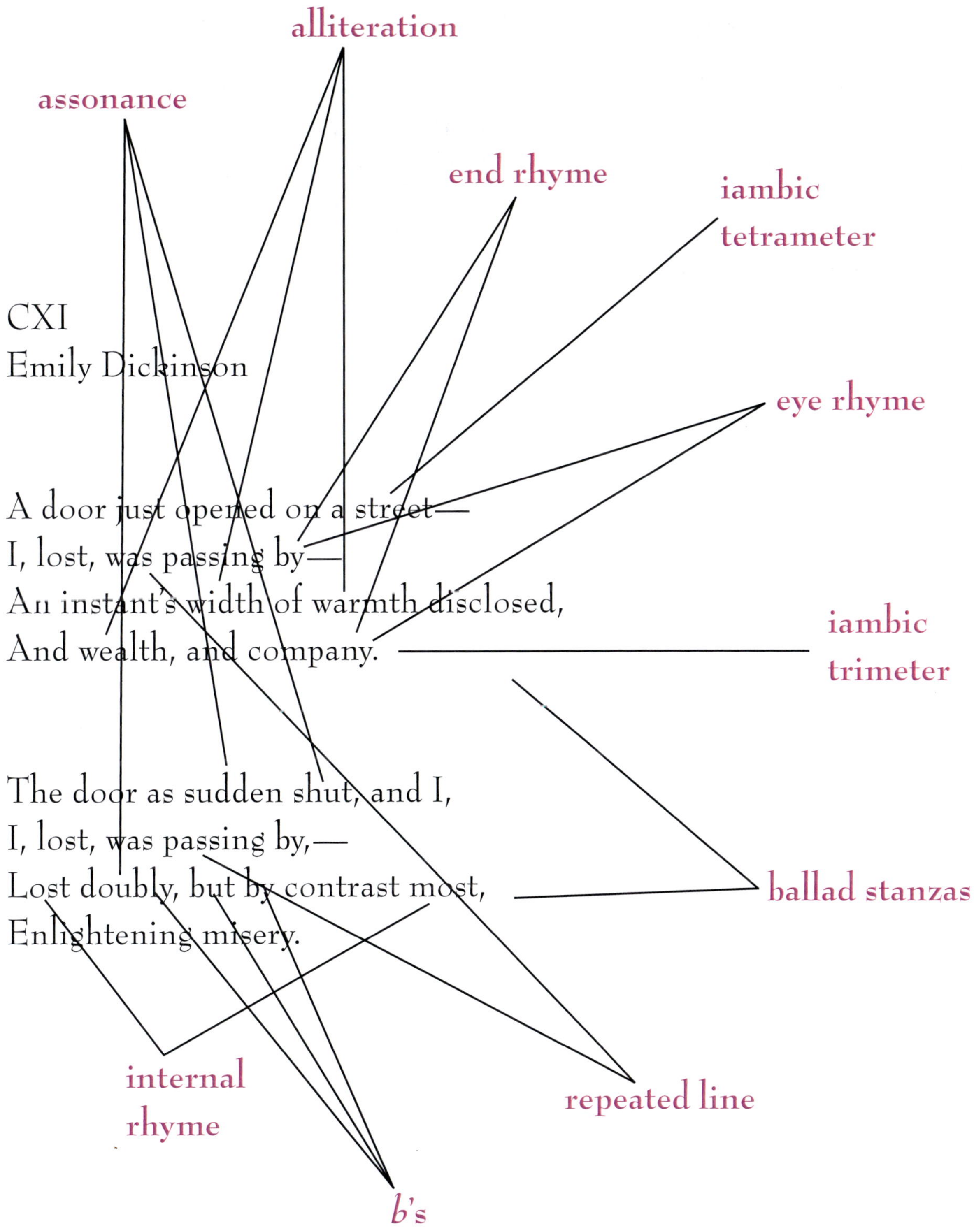

Let's invent our own stanza!

There are many different kinds of stanzas. Ballads have four lines, sonnets fourteen, limericks five, and rime royal seven. Some stanza lines are iambic pentameter, some are iambic tetrameter, and some are anapestic. The possibilities are almost endless. Let's invent our own stanza, describe its meter, assign it a rhyme scheme, and give it a name! For example, we might invent a three-line stanza, *aaa*, that is trochaic tetrameter in the first two lines and trochaic trimeter in the third. We could call it the San Juan stanza. Here is a poem that has four San Juans (the Spanish word *gente* means people and is pronounced HENtay; *calle* is pronounced CAHyay; *madre*, MAHdray, means mother; and *vida* means life and is pronounced VEEdah):

In the old street, ancient footprints
on the stones, invisible since
gente passed there. Recent

architecture's different—fewer
arches, larger spaces, newer
doorways—old things truer.

Walk along the Spanish *calle*
under balconies that saw a
different world.... Ah, *madre*,

what a scene you must have seen here
in this street, a *vida*—somewhere
ancient souls still gather.

The New Colossus
Emma Lazarus
Not like the brazen giant of Greek fame,
With conquering limbs astride from land to land;
Here at our sea-washed, sunset gates shall stand
A mighty woman with a torch, whose flame
Is the imprisoned lightning, and her name
Mother of Exiles. From her beacon-hand
Glows world-wide welcome; her mild eyes command
The air-bridged harbor that twin cities frame.
"Keep ancient lands, your storied pomp!" cries she
With silent lips. "Give me your tired, your poor,
Your huddled masses yearning to breathe free,
The wretched refuse of your teeming shore.
Send these, the homeless, tempest-tost to me,
I lift my lamp beside the golden door!"

figures
of speech
4

Figures of Speech

Poets orchestrate the array of sounds in poems. They build poems with meter, stanza, rhyme, alliteration, assonance, and consonance. They echo sounds in nature. They use language as the music of the mind.

But they also use special techniques that let them make an art of ideas.

Indirect observation, through comparison, is one of the most important techniques.

Perhaps the most common devices of comparison in poetry are the simile and the metaphor.

A simile is a comparison that is expressed directly, using a word such as *like* or *as* to indicate its nature. In a metaphor we don't use such words; we just say that something is something else.

"Liberty is like a woman with a torch" is a simile.
"Liberty is a woman with a torch" is a metaphor.

si

m

In his poem "To an Athlete Dying Young,"
A.E. Housman wanted to describe a graveyard;
he used a metaphor:

Today, the road all runners come,
Shoulder-high we bring you home,
And set you at your threshold down,
Townsman of a stiller town.

Christina Rossetti wrote:
"My heart is like
a singing bird...,"
a lovely simile.

mile

etaphor

Now we understand
what Thomas Hardy was doing
in his 1900 poem "The Darkling Thrush."
He was using a simile. Notice Hardy's
assonance on the *i* sound and his
scratchy consonants:

I leant upon a coppice gate
When frost was spectre-gray,
And Winter's dregs made desolate
The weakening eye of day.
The tangled bine-stems scored the sky
Like strings of broken lyres,
And all mankind that haunted nigh
had sought their household fires.

SIMILE

METAPHOR

And we understand
what Walt Whitman was doing
in "Song of Myself" when he used
this metaphor:

A child said, *What is the grass?* fetching
it to me with full hands; How could I
answer the child? I do not know
what it is any more than he.
I guess **it must be the flag**
of my disposition, out of hopeful green
stuff woven.

Here are two **similes** by George Gordon, Lord Byron, describing a great army, from a poem called "The Destruction of Sennacherib." When you think about what these similes mean, does that help you to imagine the scene more vividly?

And the sheen of their spears
was like stars on the sea,
when the blue wave rolls
nightly on deep Galilee.

Like the leaves of the forest
when summer is green,
that host with their banners
at sunset were seen.

like stars on the sea

Why did Byron say the stars *on the sea*? Why did he not say "the stars in the sky" and then rhyme with the noun *sky*? What difference does this idea make?

PERSONIFICATION

Another figure of speech is **personification**, which is a form of metaphor. We **personify** when we describe an object or idea as though it were a person. Do you remember Emily Dickinson saying that a "narrow wind" had complained all day how someone treated "him"? That is personification; the wind is not a person, but she imagined the wind as a person and gave us a new awareness of the hidden wind whirling in the eaves and at the windows. The Statue of Liberty is a form of personification, portraying liberty as a woman with a torch, lighting the path for immigrants arriving in America. In "The Walrus and the Carpenter," Lewis Carroll used personification:

The sun was shining on the sea,
Shining with all his might;
He did his very best to make
The billows smooth and bright—
And this was odd, because it was
The middle of the night.

The moon was shining sulkily,
Because she thought the sun
Had got no business to be there
After the day was done—
It's very rude of him," she said,
"To come and spoil the fun!"

She is solitary,
lone—not lost—
loyally she stands her post,
illuminating looming hosts
of rock with long repose,
a talent for balance,
a point of view.
True, she is solitary,
lone—not lost.

APOSTROPHE

Sometimes poets compose words that speak to someone who is absent, or to someone who is imaginary, or to an idea that is personified. Addressing someone not there in this way is called apostrophe. When President Abraham Lincoln was assassinated, a grieving Walt Whitman wrote one of the great poems of American letters, using apostrophe as the driving figure of speech. In the poem, Whitman addressed the fallen president as the captain of the ship, the nation:

O CAPTAIN! my Captain! our fearful trip is done,
The ship has weather'd every rack, the prize we sought is won,
The port is near, the bells I hear, the people all exulting,
While follow eyes the steady keel, the vessel grim and daring;
  But O heart! heart! heart!
  O the bleeding drops of red!
  Where on the deck my Captain lies,
  Fallen cold and dead.

One of the most famous poems to use apostrophe is "Ode to the West Wind," by Percy Shelley. With powerful imagination, Shelley addresses the wind:

> O wild West Wind, thou breath of Autumn's being—
> Thou from whose unseen presence the leaves dead
> Are driven, like ghosts from an enchanter fleeing,

Shelley begs the wind to be his own spirit and to blow his poetic ideas, like fallen leaves, across the world:

> Be thou, Spirit fierce,
> My spirit! be thou me, impetuous one!
> Drive my dead thoughts over the universe,
> Like wither'd leaves, to quicken a new birth;
> And, by the incantation of this verse,
> Scatter, as from an unextinguish'd hearth
> Ashes and sparks, my words among mankind!

Apostrophe to Mist, Personified

Michael Clay Thompson

Cold Ocean Mist,
stretch not your old hands to this shore,
but hold, and let the wave ranks roll alone,
and break like aches with motion, hiss and roar,
and fold and spray the salted stones.
Go, shun the soaking coast,
hold back, you gray and whispered thing,
you creeping rumor, pastel fake. I sing:
what view have you of what we are,
with lives of thought and hope bought dear?
What view have you of waits, you bearded
ghost? Hold back—stay from the window glass,
the shingled eave, the tight side-boards nailed fast.
Look not inside, come not too close,
be not here, you clouded ghost,
but slink away, withdraw with iffy whispered wisp.
We'll see the ocean, blue, when you dismiss.

APOSTROPHE & PERSONIFICATION

What is the difference between personification and apostrophe? In Shelley's "Ode to the West Wind," isn't that personification? Actually, you can have neither, either, or both. We have personification whenever we treat something that is not a person as a person. It is not apostrophe until we speak directly to someone, whether that someone is a real person (not personified) or an idea, object, or animal personified. Some silly examples:

Personification without apostrophe:

> The brilliant chicken scratched cryptic ciphers.

Apostrophe without personification:

> O, Whitman, where is thy clucky chicken now?

Apostrophe and personification:

> O, Chicken, hast thou ne'er read words?

Let's have some apostrophe fun!

Think of a common object. Something with no real dignity. A smudge on paper, or a bad-hair-day head. Something that has humor potential. Then write an apostrophe to the object, imploring it to shed its greatness upon you. Write the poem in iambic meter, with end rhyme, to make it sound formal. That should be funny! If you want, you can add archaic language like *thee* and *thy* and *thou*, use old-fashioned convoluted grammar, and even make goofy rhymes that you would never put in a serious poem.

O Bitten Pencil

Michael Clay Thompson

O bitten Pencil, all your tooth dents beauteous,
So straight thy line and gray, so gray, thy mark,
I'd gladly sing thee songs so true and fluteous,
And praise thy yellow sides, eraser dark.
How oft the words do issue forth from thee,
In curling script, undipped in ink, and gray;
How oft your soft and leaden point disjoints,
And sharper is as sharper does, I say.
But now your length is not what 'twas of yore,
When long you looked and promised even more,
You're just an inch from head to toe, you know,
And soon—into the basket I'll you throw.

CIII
Emily Dickinson

The moon was but a chin of gold
A night or two ago,
And now she turns her perfect face
Upon the world below.

hin
gold

In Shakespeare's play *Julius Caesar*,
written in poetry,
Brutus and Cassius plot to assassinate Caesar.
In act I, scene ii, Cassius vents his
resentment of Caesar's power and prestige
using a **simile**.
A *colossus* is a giant statue,
such as the Statue of Liberty.

Why, man, he doth bestride
the narrow world
Like a Colossus, and we petty men
Walk under his huge legs and peep about
To find ourselves dishonourable graves.

1	2	3	4	5
Why, man, /	he doth /	bestride /	the nar /	row world

e like like like like like like like like like like like like like lik

I.ii.

he doth bestride the narrow world like a Colossus

Colossus

ike like like like like like like like like like like like like like l

from "The Lighthouse"
Henry Wadsworth Longfellow

The rocky ledge runs far into the sea,
and on its outer point, some miles away,
the lighthouse lifts its massive masonry,
A pillar of fire by night, of cloud by day.

Enjambed or End-Stopped?

One of the most important techniques
in poetry involves what happens at the ends
of the lines. We already know that
poetry often—not always—has end rhyme
at the ends of the lines.

But what if we stopped the poem at every rhyme?

Sometimes at the ends of the lines
right after the rhyme, we see commas
or periods; in other words, there is a pause
or a stop right on the rhyme, and this
calls attention to the rhyme. It makes
the rhyme bigger, in a sense—easier to hear.
In this case, we say the line is end-stopped.

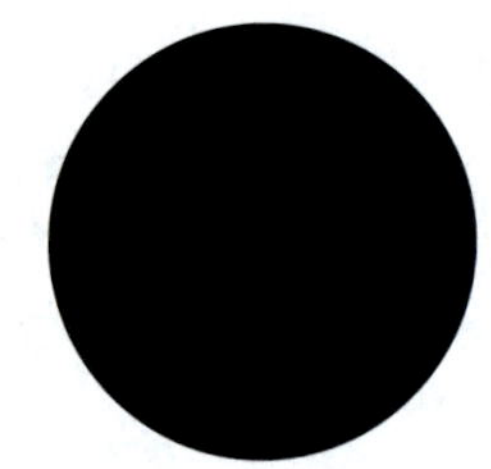

If the poem does not stop to acknowledge
the rhyme, but keeps going, and if the periods
or commas occur elsewhere, inside the lines,
this submerges the rhymes, hiding them in the
clutter of other words. We then would say that
the line is enjambed.

Enjambed

END-STOPPED

"Hee," chuckled the chicken, chomping the cheese,
"I'd rather be bubbled in juice."
"Yes," stressed the late-o tomato, "but please"—
"You shouldn't be thinking so loose!"

ENJAMBED

The absentee chicken sent seventy-three
long letters to animals seeking free
manuals. Each was a stab at
expressing thoughts clearly—good habit!

John Keats used **enjambment** in his poem "Endymion":

A thing of beauty is a joy forever:
Its loveliness increases; it will never
Pass into nothingness but still will keep
A bower quiet for us, and a sleep
Full of sweet dreams, and health,
and quiet breathing.

These are **couplets**—two-line stanzas—of iambic meter. By enjambing the lines, Keats makes the poem sound like talking, like a thoughtful conversation. The end rhymes are muted, less noticeable than they would be if the poem stopped on the rhymes. When we read, "It will never pass into nothingness," we don't even notice the end rhyme on *never*.

This nursery rhyme "The Kilkenny Cats"
is **end-stopped**. Notice how obvious the rhymes are:

There once were two cats of Kilkenny.
Each thought there was one cat too many;
So they fought and they fit,
And they scratched and they bit,
Till, excepting their nails,
And the tips of their tails,
Instead of two cats, there weren't any.

Here we also have couplets, but in this case the rhymes shout at us. They are impossible to miss because we stop the poem at each rhyme, bringing it to the fore.

Robert Frost used enjambment
in the first stanza of his 1915
poem "The Road Not Taken."
Notice the quality this gives the poem:

Two roads diverged in a yellow wood,
And sorry I could not travel both
And be one traveler, long I stood
And looked down one as far as I could
To where it bent in the undergrowth.

As we see from the complete poem on the next page, Frost built the poem from four quintets. He used end rhyme, and most lines are end-stopped. He also avoided perfect regular meter, preferring to give the poem some of the qualities of natural speech. Frost alternated back and forth, enjambing some lines and end-stopping others. How would you describe the effect he achieved by using both endings?

The Road Not Taken

Robert Frost

Two roads diverged in a yellow wood,
And sorry I could not travel both
And be one traveler, long I stood
And looked down one as far as I could
To where it bent in the undergrowth.

Then took the other, as just as fair,
And having perhaps the better claim,
Because it was grassy and wanted wear;
Though as for that the passing there
Had worn them really about the same.

And both that morning equally lay
In leaves no step had trodden black.
Oh, I kept the first for another day!
Yet knowing how way leads on to way,
I doubted if I should ever come back.

I shall be telling this with a sigh
Somewhere ages and ages hence:
Two roads diverged in a wood, and I—
I took the one less traveled by,
And that has made all the difference.

I made a tower of a chair, and climbed
to see the sight. The harbor
stretched before the lines
of buildings, boats crossed far
away, crowds breathed breaths of
haze, the sun sang glaze upon the sea
and through the glass, as free as feather
pillows—seagulls, billows, beagles, dry docks,
workers with their office woes,
regal hot dog vendors, squirrels,
clouds in loudness, buses, blocks
of sunshine on the floor. Curls
of smoke rose in the sky, crews of crows,
and sidewalks like a checker board
for sneakers, kids, and toes—
through my windows.

Let's write a poem!

Write a poem that does not sound like a poem. First, make it regular iambic tetrameter or pentameter, but in each line add one extra unstressed syllable. Then, give the poem end rhyme, but don't make perfect rhymes; make them what is called **near rhyme** or **slant rhyme**: words that almost, but not quite, rhyme, such as *float* and *pot*, or *wobble* and *bubble*, or *row* and *raw*. Finally, make the whole poem enjambed so that there is never a pause at the end rhyme. Be sure to use some of the techniques we have discussed, such as assonance or consonance, metaphor or apostrophe. An example:

Mont Saint Michel
Michael Clay Thompson

They built the castle on a small island off
the coast. A Benedictine abbey with
a spire that soars—a spear—above
the town. At low tide the sea gives
way, recedes, and mud circles the island,
but when the sea comes back, the town's
waved in again, and then a thousand
sea birds flock for fish, and caw, and down
they plunge—splash!—for briny breakfast.
On the mainland people think, and wonder
what their tiny lives would be, at last,
if they lived on the island, one day.

from "Stanzas Written on the Road between Florence and Pisa"
George Gordon, Lord Byron
Oh, talk not to me of a name great in story;
The days of our youth are the days of our glory;
And the myrtle and ivy of sweet two-and-twenty
Are worth all your laurels, though ever so plenty.

poetry
6

Building Poems

Poems are built—like buildings.

As we learn more about poems, we see that poems are built, planned, designed. Poems are built from materials: words, syllables, meter, rhymes, alliteration, assonance, consonance, metaphors, similes, personification, apostrophe. Poets use trochees, dactyls, and anapests. They often match the sounds of the poem to the ideas of the poem, like a soundtrack in a movie.

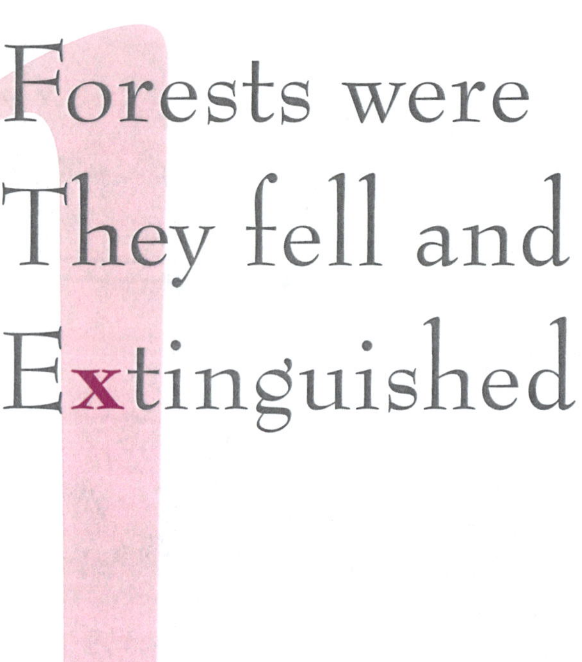

George Gordon, Lord Byron, who was a good friend of poet Percy Shelley and his wife Mary Shelley, once wrote a poem called "Darkness," using the crackly sound of the consonant *k* to create the sound of a great fire:

set on fire—but hour by hour
faded—and the crackling trunks
with a crash—and all was black.

Not only did Byron use alliteration and consonance to amplify the *k* sound, he also used alliteration in *fell* and *faded* to suggest the *fffff* sound of falling trees, and assonance in *and*, *crackling*, *crash*, and *black*. Notice the iambic pentameter:

1	2	3	4	5
Ex tin /	guished with /	a crash /	and all /	was black

Ralph Waldo Emerson used
many interesting techniques in
this stanza of his apostrophe to "The Humble-Bee."

Burly, dozing, humble-bee
Where thou art is clime for me.
Let them sail for Porto Rique,
Far-off heats through seas to seek;
I will follow thee alone,
Thou animated torrid-zone!
Zigzag steerer, desert cheerer,
Let me chase thy waving lines;
Keep me nearer, me thy hearer,
Singing over shrubs and vines.

It is an end-stopped masterpiece. Without using the word *buzz*, Emerson captured the sound of the bee's buzzing not only with a crowd of *z*'s, *v*'s, and *th*'s but also by cleverly using words such as *lines* and *vines* in which the *s* sounds like *z*.

Notice internal rhyme in *steerer* and *nearer*, the assonance in *heats, seas, seek*. What is the end rhyme scheme?

dozing, zone,

thou, thy, thee, them, thou, thy, t

zigzag, vines,

lines, waving,

desert

Poems are built.

We have just scratched the surface
of what is possible in poetry.
There are lots of other things that poets
know about, art-tricks they play
that we never even notice.

In Emerson's poem about the bee,
did you notice that Emerson used
Far-off in line four and *follow* in line
five? There we have a sound reversal:
off, follow. With soft touches like
this, a great poet can build a
structure of sounds that has an
effect on us, whether we are consciously
aware of it or not.

Dylan Thomas once said that
the "world is never the same,
once a good poem has been added to it."
He said a poem changes reality.
We begin to understand.
Poems are works of art that make
us different from who we were
and never again able to miss
the buzzing of the bee.

From "Locksley Hall," by Alfred, Lord Tennyson

Many a night I saw the Pleiads,
  rising thro' the mellow **shade**,
Glitter like a swarm of fire-flies
  tangled in a silver **braid**.

Tennyson explained, "Mr. Hallam said to me that the English people liked verse in trochaics, so I wrote the poem in this metre." We notice the assonance on *night, rising, like, fire, flies* and the end-stopped end rhyme of *shade* and *braid*. There is a beautiful simile comparing the star constellation of the Pleiades to a swarm of fireflies tangled in a silver braid. Tennyson uses fifteen syllables per line: seven trochees followed by a stress.

1	2	3	4	5	6	7	+
Glitter /	like a /	swarm of /	fire-flies /	tangled /	in a /	silver /	braid.

Poets can be secret about their techniques.
Here is the first stanza of Emerson's poem "The Snow Storm."
Look at all of the *i* sounds Emerson used. Why did he do that?

The Snow Storm

Ralph Waldo Emerson

Announced by all the trumpets of the sky,
Arrives the snow, and, driving o'er the fields,
Seems nowhere to alight: the whited air
Hides hills and woods, the river, and the heaven,
And veils the farmhouse at the garden's end.
The sled and traveler stopped, the courier's feet
Delayed, all friends shut out, the housemates sit
Around the radiant fireplace, enclosed
In a tumultuous privacy of storm.

Emerson avoids end rhyme. But notice *alight* and *whited* in line three, *hides hills* in line four, and *out*, *housemates,* and *around* in lines seven and eight. Notice *o'er* and *nowhere*. Notice the *a* sound in *delayed, housemates*, *radiant*, and *fireplace*. Notice that the poem is in iambic pentameter. By avoiding end rhyme, Emerson makes the poem sound almost like ordinary prose, and perhaps more approachable.

fireplace
by sky
privacy
driving
hides
whited
alight

The poems that poets build can
be amazing, and the more we become
aware of the forms and sounds and
ideas, the more poems mean to us.

The question is, Why?
Why do we love poems?
Why do we like it when we hear
iambic pentameter with end-stopped
end rhyme?

Why do we love ballad stanzas?
What is so pleasing about good
alliteration, assonance, and consonance?

Why do brilliant metaphors open our eyes?

Do we really need to know these things
in order to be well-educated?

Poems put us in touch with the rhythms of the world. Our heartbeats, the crashing surf on the shore, the patterns of bird calls, the seasons, night and day—nature is full of rhythms, and poetry reconnects our awareness of rhythm.

Poems introduce us to our voice. Our language rises and falls, has vowels and consonants, is filled with music whether we like it or not. The voices of our parents and friends are among the things we love most in life, and our own voice is among the closest part of ourselves to ourselves. But ordinarily we are so used to these voices that we no longer really hear them.

Poems are works of art in language. Many of the greatest writings—such as Homer's *Iliad*, Shakespeare's *Hamlet*, and Whitman's *Leaves of Grass*—are poems. By studying poetry, we not only learn about poems, we also educate our minds to perceive great language in other forms, such as the assonance and consonance in President Abraham Lincoln's *Gettysburg Address*:
"Four score and seven years ago, our
fathers brought forth upon this continent...."

Poetry is a big part of becoming educated.

The Cold Boat

Michael Clay Thompson

He walked across the frosty beach—
a crunchy sound, and checked the rowboat out.
Cold wood, good paint—he could reach
the oars. He pushed the boat down to
the water's edge, slow slide, the fresh waves slapped
the bow, a splashing sound and now
he pushed out, jumped in, found
the oars and pulled, the water curled
around the oars. His gear and lunch
were stowed under the plank,
the oarlocks rattled in the sun,
and suddenly a cold wind flapped
his flannel shirt, a snapping cold,
and overhead the whole blue day,
blue wind, blue sun, unfolded slowly.

Poetry to explore:

On the Grasshopper and the Cricket
John Keats

The poetry of earth is never dead:
When all the birds are faint with the hot sun,
And hide in cooling trees, a voice will run
From hedge to hedge about the new-mown mead;
That is the Grasshopper's—he takes the lead
In summer luxury,—he has never done
With his delights; for when tired out with fun
He rests at ease beneath some pleasant weed.
The poetry of earth is ceasing never:
On a lone winter evening, when the frost
Has wrought a silence, from the stove there shrills
The Cricket's song, in warmth increasing ever,
And seems to one in drowsiness half lost,
The Grasshopper's among some grassy hills.

XXIII (three of five stanzas)
Emily Dickinson

A bird came down the walk:
He did not know I saw;
He bit an angle-worm in halves
and ate the fellow, raw.

And then he drank a dew
From a convenient grass,
And then hopped sidewise to the wall
To let a beetle pass.

He glanced with rapid eyes
That hurried all abroad,—
They looked like frightened beads, I thought
He stirred his velvet head...

a convenient grass

Some Elements

Sound

Rhyme: the repetition of sound
End rhyme: rhyme at the ends of lines of poetry
Internal rhyme: rhymes inside the lines
Eye rhyme: rhymes that look alike but do not sound alike
Rhyme scheme: using letters to show the arrangement of rhyme
Onomatopoeia: a word that sounds like what it describes
Alliteration: the repetition of initial vowels or consonants
Assonance: the repetition of vowel sounds
Consonance: the repetition of consonant sounds
End-stopped: periods or commas at the ends of the lines
Enjambed: when there are no pauses at the ends of the lines

Rhythm

Meter: the pattern or rhythm of syllables
Stress: the emphasis given to certain syllables in words
Foot: the repeating unit of meter
Iamb: a two-syllable foot with the stress on the second syllable
Trochee: a two-syllable foot with the stress on the first syllable
Spondee: a two-syllable foot, both syllables stressed
Anapest: a three-syllable foot with the stress on the third
Dactyl: a three-syllable foot with the stress on the first
Iambic pentameter: five iambs to a line of ten syllables
Monometer: one foot per line
Dimeter: two feet per line
Trimeter: three feet per line

# of Poetry

Tetrameter: four feet per line
Pentameter: five feet per line
Hexameter: six feet per line
Heptameter: seven feet per line
Octameter: eight feet per line

Stanza: a part of a poem, based on form of meter and rhyme

- **Couplet**: a two-line stanza
- **Triplet**: a three-line stanza
- **Quatrain**: a four-line stanza
- **Quintet**: a five-line stanza
- **Sestet**: a six-line stanza
- **Ballad**: a quatrain alternating iambic tetrameter and iambic trimeter. The rhyme scheme of a ballad is *abcb*.
- **English sonnet**: a fourteen-line poem of four stanzas—three quatrains and a couplet. The rhyme scheme is *abab cdcd efef gg*.
- **Limerick**: a five-line nonsense poem, mostly anapest, *aabba*
- **Rime royal**: a seven-line stanza, iambic pentameter, *ababbcc*

Figures of Speech: comparisons that are not literally true

- **Simile**: an openly expressed comparison using *like* or *as*
- **Metaphor**: an implied comparison
- **Personification**: portraying an object as a person
- **Apostrophe**: addressing someone or something not present

Questions for Review

1. The words *cough* and *through* are an example of:
   a. end rhyme
   b. eye rhyme
   c. internal rhyme
   d. alliteration

2. The words *crash* and *buzz* are examples of:
   a. end rhyme
   b. eye rhyme
   c. alliteration
   d. onomatopoeia

3. When we begin words with the same sound, like *rail*, *rod*, *rip*, and *reed*, that is:
   a. eye rhyme
   b. alliteration
   c. onomatopoeia
   d. end rhyme

4. A line of iambic tetrameter has:
   a. one foot
   b. two feet
   c. three feet
   d. four feet

5. An iamb contains:
   a. one syllable
   b. two syllables
   c. three syllables
   d. four syllables

6. The word *baboon* is an example of a(n):
   a. iamb
   b. dactyl
   c. trochee
   d. anapest

7. The rhyme scheme of a ballad is:
   a. *abcd*
   b. *abcb*
   c. *abab*
   d. *abcc*

8. A ballad stanza contains:
   a. one line
   b. two lines
   c. three lines
   d. four lines

9. A ballad has iambic tetrameter in lines:
   a. two and four
   b. one and three
   c. three and five
   d. three and four

10. The words "The sheen of their spears was like stars on the sea" contain a(n):
   a. metaphor
   b. eye rhyme
   c. simile
   d. onomatopoeia

11. The words "Life is a walking shadow" contain a:
   a. metaphor
   b. ballad
   c. simile
   d. sonnet

12. A sonnet contains three quatrains and:
   a. one tercet
   b. two couplets
   c. a couplet
   d. a quintet

13. A sonnet is written in:
   a. iambic pentameter
   b. trochaic tetrameter
   c. dactylic trimeter
   d. anapestic dimeter

14. Rime royal has:
   a. four lines
   b. five lines
   c. six lines
   d. seven lines

15. Blake's line "Tiger, Tiger, burning bright" is an example of:
a. iambic meter
b. dactylic meter
c. trochaic meter
d. anapestic meter

16. A section of a poem, based on a form that repeats, is called a(n):
a. meter
b. couplet
c. alliteration
d. stanza

17. The rhyme scheme *ababbcc* is the scheme of a:
a. ballad
b. rime royal
c. limerick
d. quatrain

18. Addressing someone not present in a poem is called:
a. apostrophe
b. simile
c. metaphor
d. personification

19. A six-line stanza is called a(n):
a. quatrain
b. quintet
c. sestet
d. octet

20. Which poet addressed a poem to the west wind?
a. George Gordon, Lord Byron
b. Emily Dickinson
c. Percy Shelley
d. Alfred, Lord Tennyson

21. The line "Zigzag steerer, desert cheerer" contains:
a. eye rhyme
b. internal rhyme
c. iambics
d. alliteration

22. The line "The wind befriended me" contains:
a. personification
b. alliteration
c. simile
d. apostrophe

23. The line "Suddenly everyone opened their dinosaurs" is
a. dactylic trimeter
b. anapestic trimeter
c. dactylic tetrameter
d. anapestic tetrameter

24. The line "Whose woods these are I think I know" is
a. trochaic tetrameter
b. iambic tetrameter
c. dactylic tetrameter
d. anapestic tetrameter

25. The line "Suddenly we stopped. Dead." has a(n):
a. iamb
b. dactyl
c. spondee
d. metaphor

26. The line "Blue tunes fooled us, and you drew at noon" has:
a. assonance
b. alliteration
c. consonance
d. simile

27. The line "Particular attempts witnessed by attorneys" has:
a. assonance
b. metaphor
c. consonance
d. personification

28. The line "At the top of the stairs was a chair" is
a. iambic trimeter
b. anapestic trimeter
c. dactylic trimeter
d. trochaic trimeter

29. A four-line stanza is a:
a. quatrain
b. triplet
c. quintet
d. sestet

30. If a poem is not end-stopped, it is:
a. a quintet
b. a sonnet
c. personified
d. enjambed

from "The Walrus and the Carpenter"
Lewis Carroll

The Walrus and the Carpenter
Were walking close at hand:
They wept like anything to see
Such quantities of sand:
"If this were only cleared away,"
They said, "it would be grand!"

Marry, I cannot show it in rhyme;
I have tried: I can find out
no rhyme to 'lady' but 'baby,'
an innocent rhyme;
for 'scorn,' 'horn,' a hard rhyme;
for 'school,' 'fool,' a babbling rhyme;
very ominous endings:
no, I was not born under a
rhyming planet....

– *Much Ado About Nothing*
William Shakespeare